UNITY IN DIVERSITY

Thoughts of the world's great religions

PUBLICATIONS
Compiled, edited and transcreated
by
O.P. Ghai

SIMPLIFIED SCRIPTURES

UNITY IN DIVERSITY
with a foreword by Dr Karan Singh
(in 25 languages)
THE BHAGAVAD GITA
with a foreword by M.P. Pandit
THE JAPJI
with a foreword by Dr. Jaswant Singh Neki
SELECTIONS FROM THE QUR'AN
with a foreword by Prof. Rasheeduddin Khan
SELECTIONS FROM THE BIBLE
with a foreword by Fr. T.V. Kunnunkal

THE FINE ART OF LIVING

QUEST FOR EXCELLENCE   QUEST FOR INSPIRATION
QUEST FOR DEVELOPMENT   QUEST FOR ACHIEVEMENT
QUEST FOR PERFECTION   QUEST FOR ENLIGHTENMENT

EXCELLENCE IN WORLD RELIGIONS

EXCELLENCE IN HINDUISM
EXCELLENCE IN ISLAM
EXCELLENCE IN SIKHISM
EXCELLENCE IN JAINISM
EXCELLENCE IN BUDDHISM
EXCELLENCE IN ZOROASTRIANISM
EXCELLENCE IN BAHAI

GIFT BOOKS FOR ALL OCCASIONS

AMBITION, BEAUTY, BOOKS, BUSINESS, CHARACTER, COURAGE, DREAMS, FAME, FAITH, FRIENDSHIP, GIVING, HAPPINESS, HEALTH, HEART, KISSES, LIFE, LOVE, MUSIC, MARRIAGE, NATURE, ROMANCE, SMILE, SUCCESS, TIME, TRUTH, YOUTH, WOMEN, WORK

OTHER PUBLICATIONS

AS A MAN THINKETH *by James Allen*
RUBAIYAT OMARKHAYYAM

rendered into English verse by Edward Fitzgerald

THE STERLING BOOK OF
UNITY IN DIVERSITY

Thoughts of the world's great religions

*A guide to the understanding of the
fundamental unity underlying the great
living religions of the world*

Compiled and Edited by
O.P. Ghai

Foreword by
Dr Karan Singh

Sterling Paperbacks

STERLING PAPERBACKS
An imprint of
Sterling Publishers (P) Ltd.
A-59, Okhla Industrial Area, Phase-II,
New Delhi-110020.
Tel: 26387070, 26386209; Fax: 91-11-26383788
E-mail: sterlingpublishers@airtelbroadband.in
ghai@nde.vsnl.net.in
www.sterlingpublishers.com

The Sterling Book of Unity in Diversity
Copyright © 2008, O.P.Ghai (1919-1992)
ISBN 978-81-207-3739-6

Printed and Published by
Sterling Publishers Pvt. Ltd., New Delhi-110 020.

TO

seekers of truth, compassion and harmony,
to whatever religion they may belong.

Foreword

As we enter the 21st century, the importance of the Interfaith movement is becoming increasingly evident. If we are to establish a sane and harmonious global society on Planet Earth, we will have to get over the negative residue of fundamentalism and exclusivism that have been such a marked feature of the inter-religious scene for centuries. We have to accept the fact that the divine has not thought it necessary to have only a single religion for all humanity, and that the multiple religious traditions in the world only add to our civilisational richness and creativity. As the Rig Veda says, *Ekam sad viprah bahudha vadanti* – the Truth is one, the wise call it by many names.

This is the basic concept behind the Interfaith movement which has seen considerable activity around the world from the first *Parliament of the World's Religions* held in Chicago in 1893, the second a hundred years later, again, in Chicago in 1993, the third in Cape Town, South Africa, at the end of 1999, and the fourth in July 2004, Barcelona, Spain. In addition to these Parliaments, there have been a number of Interfaith conferences arranged by several Interfaith organisations in the 20th century. A significant event – *The Millennium World Peace Summit of Religious and Spiritual Leaders* – was held under the auspices of the United Nations in August 2000 in the main hall of the United Nations itself. I had the privilege of presiding over the first Plenary Session of this historic meeting.

One of the major Interfaith organisations is the *Temple of Understanding*, founded four decades ago by a dynamic American woman, Juliet Hollister. Over these years it has developed into a major force towards furthering Interfaith harmony and understanding and has held a number of meetings in New York and around the world, bringing together people belonging to different faiths in a creative dialogue aimed at a deeper understanding of each other's traditions. These activities now cover the twelve major faiths of the world. As Chairman of the Temple of Understanding and President of the India Chapter, I have personally been involved in this movement for several years. The India Chapter of the Temple of Understanding has held many functions in Delhi and in other parts of India, including a significant seminar on *Interfaith Education for the Global Society* in January 2002 in New Delhi.

India is par excellence a land of different religions. Four of the world's great religions–Hinduism, Jainism, Buddhism and Sikhism–were born here, and five came to us from West Asia and flourished in our land–Zoroastrianism, Judaism, Christianity, Islam and the Baha'i Faith. We are also opening up towards the three great religious traditions of East Asia – Confucianism, Taoism and Shintoism. There has been a widespread demand for a handy publication that would contain extracts from the great religions of the world upon various aspects of our inner and outer life. The late Shri O.P. Ghai, an outstanding publisher and author, had produced a small book entitled *Unity in Diversity*, which admirably fulfils this requirement. *The Hari-Tara Charitable Trust*, which my wife and I set up in memory of my parents, decided with co-operation from Shri S.K. Ghai, who manages Sterling Publishers after his father's death, to sponsor a new edition of this book.

Interfaith harmony is an essential prerequisite for the establishment of a peaceful and harmonious global society in the years and decades ahead, and it is my hope that this book will make a small but significant contribution in that direction.

New Delhi   **Karan Singh**

8

Preface

This humble compilation is not only an attempt to glean the best in living religious literatures but is also a guide to the understanding of the fundamental similarity underlying the religions. I am sure it will provide comfort, guidance and inspiration to those who go through the book.

I have been a student of comparative religion for the last fifty years, but I have felt the necessity of publishing this small volume at this particular time when religious intolerance is at its height all over the world. If this attempt can bring sanity even to one religious fanatic bent upon harming his fellow-beings simply because he believes in a different religion, I will feel amply rewarded.

This book has been thoroughly revised and enlarged by the addition of sayings from the Baha'i Faith with its emphasis on the spiritual unity of mankind. Now it contains the best of wisdom from the twelve living religions of the world.

O.P. Ghai

Great Religions of the World

BAHA'I

The Baha'i religion is the most recent of the great religions. Its founder, Baha'u' llah (1817-1892) was born in Persia and was banished to Akka in the Holy Land. He declared that the oneness of mankind is the new axis around which the spiritual and social life in an age of maturity revolves. This concept includes the oneness of God, the oneness of the religions in their origin and goal as well as the reconciliation between religion and science and their mutual cooperation.

BUDDHISM

Buddhism is the faith founded by Gautama (563-483 B.C.) who was a prince born in the Sakya clan. He gave up a life of pleasure and luxury to seek and find a solution to the universal problem of suffering, and in this context propounded his Four Noble Truths. Himself a wandering teacher for half a century, the Buddha - the Enlightened One - had a profound impact upon succeeding generations and Buddhism grew to be a major religion in South and South-East Asia.

CHRISTIANITY

Christianity grew out of Judaism and the Christians claim many of the Jewish sacred writings as their own. The Christian Bible contains both the Old Testament and the New Testament, while many editions of the Bible also include the books of the Apocrypha. The Christian Messiah, Jesus of Nazareth, was born a Jew, steeped in Jewish tradition and culture. The next step for Jesus and his followers was to break away from the narrow nationalism of the Judaism of the past and to carry the high ethical idealism of the greatest of the prophets to all people, whether Jew or non-Jew. Christianity, growing out of the teachings of Jesus of Nazareth, developed into a religious movement in the Roman Empire. Its missionary activities have carried it to all parts of the globe.

CONFUCIANISM

Confucius, its founder, thought of his work not as a religious text but as a social and administrative treatise. China had been religious long before Confucius, who lived between 551 and 478 B.C. In fact, from its earliest days, about 2356 B.C., China has had an official religion. During the later part of the sixth century B.C., however, the government was falling into decay and the moral life of the people was degenerating. It was at that time that the young Confucius became famous as a teacher. This was followed by his success in political office and then as an itinerant preacher. As a result of his works and life, the religion of China, which had existed for centuries, became known as Confucianism.

HINDUISM

Hinduism is the oldest persisting religion in the world, dating back many thousands of years to the dawn of civilization. Despite a wide variety of beliefs and practices, Hinduism has always retained certain core beliefs regarding the nature of the soul and its relationship with the Divine flowing from the Vedas and the Upanishads. It has also undergone a constant process of reform and renaissance down through the centuries, and has produced great seers and sages, scholars and seekers for the truth.

ISLAM

Islam is one of the world's most widespread religions. With the exceptions of Sikhism and Baha'i, it is the newest of the world's great religions, dating from the Hegira or flight of the Prophet from Mecca in A.D. 622. Mohammed, its founder, was born in A.D. 570 at Mecca, the chief city of Arabia. Mecca became the hub of a great wheel of Mohammedan faith from which spokes radiated in every direction.

JAINISM

Hinduism was, in its earlier phases, dominated by caste distinctions, animal sacrifice and other such practices. These offended a great many sensitive people in India who eventually sought for reforms. Jainism was the first organised effort to effect such reform.

JUDAISM

Judaism is the name for the religion of the Hebrews. This religion, in its long development from before 1200 B.C., has borrowed a great deal from other religions but has also contributed greatly to many religious systems, particularly Christianity and Islam. Indeed, Christianity, grew out of Judaism and includes the sacred writings of Judaism in its own sacred literature.

SHINTOISM

Shinto is the national religion of Japan. According to some authorities, it represents the distinctive religious genius of Japan from the very beginning of its history. Others, while recognizing its deep significance for Japanese life, argue that it is in no sense a religion but is rather a patriotic cult. Whether we call it a religion or not, it has definitely made a significant contribution to the political theory and national stability of Japan.

SIKHISM

Sikhism is among the most modern of great living religions. Its founder, Nanak, lived between A.D. 1469 and 1538 in the province of Punjab in India. His teachings are infused with love and compassion. Though it has a small number of adherents, Sikhism has exerted considerable influence upon the religious life of the East.

TAOISM

Taoism is the oldest of the personally founded religions of China, being one of the "Three Religions" of that vast land. The other two are Confucianism and Buddhism. However, there are many who maintain that it should not be classed as a religion at all. Others point out that it was originally simply a way of ethical living and was not organised as a religion until late in its history, close to the beginning of the Christian era.

ZOROASTRIANISM

The history of Zoroastrianism reveals that it has had a profound influence over other religions, particularly Christianity. Today its followers are in existence scattered throughout Persia and India. A great many of the concepts found both in the Old and in the New Testament stem directly from Zoroastrianism, though the religion itself is not mentioned anywhere in the Bible.

Contents

Major Sacred Writings of the World's Great Religions from which selections have been made

I. Hinduism
The Rig Veda
The Upanishads
The Bhagavad Gita

II. Zoroastrianism
The Yasna
The Vendidad

III. Taoism
The Tao Teh King
The Writings of Kwang-Tze

IV. Confucianism
The Shu King
The Shih King
The Lun Yu
The Chung Yung
The Meng-Tge

V. Jainism
The Ayaranya Sutra
The Sutrakritanga
The Uttaradhyayana Sutra

VI. Buddhism
The Vinaya Pitaka
The Sutta Pitaka
The Dhammapada

VII. Judaism
The Old Testament
The Apocrypha

VIII. Christianity
The New Testament

IX. Islam
The Koran

X. Shintoism
The Kojiki
Selected Materials

XI. Sikhism
The Guru Granth
The Japji
Asa Di War
The Rahiras

XII. Baha'i
Gleanings from the
writings of Baha'u'llah
Baha'i World Faith
Writings of Baha'u'llah–
A Compilation selections
from the writings of
Abdu'l-Baha'

ANGER

One should not give way to anger, but should control it. He who controls anger has power far greater than those who give way to it. The one is master of his emotion while the other is mastered by it. Hatred is damaging to mankind and should be eliminated.

BUDDHISM

God does not sanction anger. One should be slow to anger and always ready to forgive. If one hates his "brother" he is like a murderer. The mark of a Christian is love, not hatred.

CHRISTIANITY

One should so conduct himself as to avoid hatred or anger from others. Mild speech and demanding little of others are ways to avoid their anger.

CONFUCIANISM

Anger breeds confusion. He who would be clear and unconfused must avoid becoming angry.

HINDUISM

Abu Huraira reported God's messenger as saying: "The strong man is not the good wrestler; the strong man is only he who controls himself when he is angry."

ISLAM

Anger is not for the wise or the religious. They will endure persecution and not be angry. Only the ignorant and the sinful will give way to anger.

JAINISM

Love and not anger, is commended. Anger causes strife and destruction. One should respond to anger in others with love and kindness. That way he will turn away the anger of others. Only fools give way to anger.

JUDAISM

Avarice is a dog,
Falsehood a sweeper,
Cheating is the eating of a dead body;
Slander is the dirt that my tongue tasteth,
And anger is the fire that burns me as at cremation,
I indulge in nothing but self-esteem;
See, these are my doings, O Lord

SIKHISM

No one should be angry with holy men since they are not angry with anyone. Return anger with goodness. Do good to those who hate you.

TAOISM

21

Never give way to the deadly emotions of Anger,
Envy, Fear, and Grief. Always be Optimistic.

ZOROASTRIANISM

Never become angry with one another ... Love the
creatures for the sake of God and not for themselves.
You will never become angry or impatient
if you love them for the sake of God.

BAHA'I

BROTHERHOOD

A friend is a great treasure and should be cherished as a brother. One should make good men his closest friends, his brothers.

BUDDHISM

All men are brothers. If one has anything against one's brother, he should make his peace with him before attending to other religious duties. As one treats a brother, so does he treat God. To hate one's brother is evil. Brotherly love should rule the world.

CHRISTIANITY

Friendship and brotherhood are the cardinal virtues. One should gather about many friends and should love them as brothers. The wise man will choose friends worthy of brotherly love.

CONFUCIANISM

The good man makes no distinction between friend and foe, brother and stranger, but regards them all with impartiality. A true friend will be sympathetic to you at all times.

HINDUISM

All mankind is one family, one people. All men are
brothers and should live as such. The Lord loves
those who so live.

ISLAM

Be fair and impartial to all. Treat all men as
brothers at all times. As one treats men, so should
he treat all animals. They are also our brothers.

JAINISM

God has made all men brothers and they should
live together as brothers at all times. It is good
for men to act in unity as brothers. Such action
will be blessed by God and will prosper.

JUDAISM

Heaven is the father and earth the mother of all
men. Therefore, all men are brothers and should
dwell together as such. By so living the country
will be free from hate and sorrow.

SHINTO

Get together my brethren and remove
all misunderstandings through regard for each other.

SIKHISM

The spirit of brotherhood, kindness is necessary if one would win friends. The spirit of the market, where men sell goods, should not be the spirit of the good man.

TAOISM

One's friends should be holy people. A holy man will radiate holiness to all his friends.

ZOROASTRIANISM

It beseemeth all men, in this Day, to take firm hold on the Most Great Name, and to establish the unity of all mankind. There is no place to flee to, no refuge that anyone can seek, except Him.

BAHA'I

COURAGE

*The wise man is not afraid. He knows his strength
and does not fear. Likewise, he knows his
weaknesses and does not attempt the impossible.*

BUDDHISM

*God is strong, the helper of the good. Therefore,
we should not fear, but face life with courage and
confidence that the source of all power in the
universe is on our side. God watches over even
the weakest of men.*

CHRISTIANITY

*The man of principle is courageous. He knows the
right and will fight for it at all costs. God is on
his side, and he takes courage from the knowledge
of this fact.*

CONFUCIANISM

*To realize that God is all and all is God gives man
courage. He does not shrink.*

HINDUISM

God will guide the good. Therefore, they shall have no fear. He will lead them through all the rough spots of life.

ISLAM

A man may conquer thousands and thousands of invincible foes but that is of no real consequence; his greatest victory is when he conquers only his own self through indomitable courage.

JAINISM

Be courageous, for God will not fail you. The Lord is on the side of the righteous man, whom then shall he fear? He will give you the strength you need when the time arrives for it.

JUDAISM

Brave is he, who possessing strength displays it not,
and lives in humble ways.
He is brave,
Who fights for the down-trodden.

SIKHISM

The philosopher is not influenced by praise or blame. He knows the truth and is not afraid, regardless of what happens to him in this world.

TAOISM

Courage begets strength by struggle with hardships. Courage grows from fighting danger and overcoming obstacles. Develop the courage to act according to your convictions, to speak what is true, and to do what is Right.

ZOROASTRIANISM

The source of courage and power is the promotion of the Word of God, and steadfastness in His Love.

BAHA'I

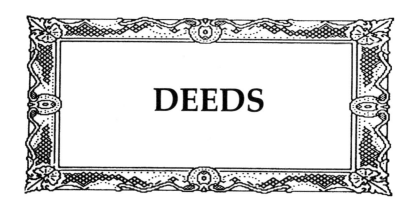

DEEDS

Deeds determine one's place in society. One becomes an outcast or a highly placed person by his deeds. Evil deeds are easy to do; good deeds are difficult; but the good deeds pay the highest rewards.

BUDDHISM

Man is known by his deeds, and is judged even so by God. God will reward good deeds and punish evil ones. To profess goodness is of no value; one must do good deeds or be condemned.

CHRISTIANITY

Reward will follow every good deed. Only by doing good deeds can a man know the true joy of living and have a long life.

CONFUCIANISM

One becomes what one does. The doer of good deeds will become good and the doer of evil deeds will become evil. Action, the doing of the good, is superior to renunciation. Thus, at all times one should be doing good.

HINDUISM

On the Day of Judgement every soul shall be judged in accordance with his deeds. To do good drives out evil.

ISLAM

The good show the way to others by their good acts. Each day passes never to return. Therefore, do good at all times, for you can never call back a day to perform a good deed that was not done.

JAINISM

Do good at all times, for man will be judged by his works.

JUDAISM

Man's deeds are recorded by the divine. He becomes good in the eyes of the divine by doing good deeds. God is the source of good deeds.

SIKHISM

We come to the Wise One through good deeds. It is important that we keep ourselves physically fit to do good deeds at all times.

ZOROASTRIANISM

*It behoves each one of you to manifest the attributes
of God, and to exemplify by your deeds and
words the signs of His righteousness, His power
and glory.*

BAHA'I

DUTY

One should be faithful to his duty at all times regardless of the situation. Faithfulness to duty brings the greatest of rewards.

BUDDHISM

One has a duty to God and duties towards one's fellows. One should take care to discharge one's duties. It is one's duty at all times to do the will of God.

CHRISTIANITY

Man's duty comes from Heaven. Therefore, he fails in his duty at his peril. The wise man makes duty his aim at all times.

CONFUCIANISM

Never falter in doing your duty. God has decreed man's duty, and to fail is to disobey God. It is through duty that a man reaches perfection.

HINDUISM

All men who do their duty will receive a fitting reward from the Lord.

ISLAM

A wise man discovers his duty and does it at all costs. It is the duty of all to be impartial and to abstain from causing injury to all living things.

JAINISM

The whole duty of man is to fear God and keep His commandments. This involves love and service to God with one's whole heart.

JUDAISM

The path of duty is near at hand, men seek it in what is remote.

SHINTO

He alone is a householder who disciplines his sense desires. And begs from God Contemplation, Austerity and Self-control. And gives in charity all he can through his body.

SIKHISM

The middle way is the duty of man. He should avoid all excess. In this way he fulfills his duty toward man and God.

TAOISM

*The duty and good works which a son performs
are as much the father's as though they had been
done by his own hand.*

ZOROASTRIANISM

*That one indeed is a man who, today, dedicateth
himself to the service of the entire human race.*

BAHA'I

EVIL

Evil actions will be punished inevitably, and good actions rewarded with happiness. The good man will loathe evil at all times and will keep himself pure.

BUDDHISM

The Christian will hate evil and will keep himself free even from the appearance of evil. To know what is good and not to do it is sin.

CHRISTIANITY

Heaven visits punishment or happiness upon man in accordance with his good or evil acts. The rewards of goodness are inevitable, just as are the punishments of evil.

CONFUCIANISM

He who is evil cannot hope to attain eternal happiness. Heaven punishes the evil. All pain and suffering comes from evildoing.

HINDUISM

Avoid all evil. One may commit evil by doing something wrong or by approving another's evil act. Do not cause others to sin.

JAINISM

Evil is the cause of suffering. Everyone is evil and must repent. God will reward those who flee from evil and seek the good. God is ever ready to pardon.

JUDAISM

After three years an evil becomes a necessity. See no evil, hear no evil, speak no evil.

SHINTO

When the clothes are soiled and rendered impure,
They are cleansed with soap,
When the mind is defiled by sin
It is rendered pure by the love of his Nam.

Call them the evil spirits,
Who are engrossed in Maya, lust, anger and pride,
Call him an evil spirit who does evil actions,
And knows not the Master.

Remove sin from your heart,
And serve others.

By remembering God,
All your sins shall be washed off.

SIKHISM

41

Those who do evil in the open light of day – men will punish them. Those who do evil in secret – God will punish them. Who fears both man and God, he is fit to walk alone.

TAOISM

When a man makes an honest effort to cleanse himself day by day of his evil thoughts, evil words, and evil deeds, then will follow in their wake, as the day the night, good thoughts, good words, and good deeds.

ZOROASTRIANISM

The source of all evil is for man to turn away from his Lord and to set his heart on things ungodly. In all matters, moderation is desirable. If a thing is carried to excess, it will prove a source of evil.

BAHA'I

FAITH

Faith is necessary for the virtuous life. One's faith will not go unrewarded. Prosperity follows upon faith.

BUDDHISM

Faith is necessary, but it must be accompanied by works. One who is faithful even to death will receive a crown of life. He who asks in perfect faith shall receive. Faith is basic to full understanding.

CHRISTIANITY

He who lacks faith will not succeed. One must hold to faith at all times. Heaven makes great demands upon one's faith, but God is with man and he should never waver in his faith.

CONFUCIANISM

Faith is the pathway to wisdom. This faith will come if one yearns in his heart for it. The most prized of God is the man of faith.

HINDUISM

Man should have faith in God, for God will always prove faithful. But God has no patience with the unfaithful.

ISLAM

The man of faith has chosen the right pathway.
He should practise his faith at all times.

JAINISM

God is faithful and will preserve the faithful. The
man of faith can expect great rewards from God.

JUDAISM

Even the slightest yielding to doubt is a departing
from the nature of man. Faith is fundamental
to human beings.

SHINTO

Good life and immortality are the rewards of the
faithful. The religion of the Wise One will
cleanse the faithful from all sin.

SIKHISM

To have less than enough faith is to have no faith
at all. The divine will repay faith with faith and
faithlessness with faithlessness.

TAOISM

Those who believe,
Their minds awaken to higher consciousness.
And to the inner knowledge of all spheres.

ZOROASTRIANISM

The essence of faith is fewness of words and
abundance of deeds; he whose words exceed his deeds,
know verily his death is better than his life.

BAHA'I

FAMILY

The aged should be respected and revered. He who does this will receive great rewards and will prosper. Children should give support to their parents. Always honour one's parents.

BUDDHISM

Children must respect and obey their parents, but the parents must also respect their children. There is to be mutual understanding and appreciation within the family.

CHRISTIANITY

Filial piety is highly respected. The virtuous man will never neglect his parents. Love and respect for relations and elders is the beginning of love and respect for all members of the state.

CONFUCIANISM

Love and respect must reign in the home. This is commended because every member of the household is a soul and as a soul he is worthy of love and respect. Faithfulness must mark the relationship of husband and wife.

HINDUISM

A child should be grateful both to God and to his parents. The family is a unit, and should beseech God as one.

ISLAM

The child should support his parents when he is able to do so. Although the family should work together to aid each other, each one must suffer for his own deeds. One's family is of no use to him at the time of judgement. Then he shall be judged in accordance with his deeds.

JAINISM

Family love and solidarity is basic to Jewish life. The child must honour and respect his parents and obey them at all times. The parents must teach the child and rear him in the ways of the Lord.

JUDAISM

Son, why do you quarrel with your father due to him you have grown to this age. It is a sin to argue with him. Always look up to the Highest, living among your kith and kin, Like the lotus that stands above its roots which are in mud.

SIKHISM

Obedience, peace, charity, humility, truth, and righteousness should prevail in every home and the children should respect the parents at all times.

ZOROASTRIANISM

If love and agreement are manifest in a single family, that family will advance, become illumined and spiritual.

BAHA'I

FORGIVENESS

*Whatsoever may be the cause of your suffering,
do not wound another, forgive him.*

BUDDHISM

*Man should be forgiving. As he forgives his
fellow beings so God will forgive him. God is
forgiving and is ready and anxious to forgive
those who ask for His forgiveness.*

CHRISTIANITY

*One should forgive if the act is unintentional, but
should punish the intended evil act.*

CONFUCIANISM

*God will forgive the sinner, if he earnestly casts
away his sin. Human forgiveness is the way to
happiness among men. A wise man will always be
ready to forgive.*

HINDUISM

*God loves those who forgive their fellow beings
God is forgiving and is anxious to forgive all
those who will come to Him with contrite hearts.*

ISLAM

*I forgive all the living beings. All living beings
may forgive me. I cherish friendly feelings
towards all. I do not hold any ill will towards man,
beast or plant.*

JAINISM

*The Lord forgives all sins. He is forgiving at all
times, if the wicked ones will forsake their ways.*

JUDAISM

Forgive others but yourself never.

SHINTO

*Countless people have perished, Without the
spirit of forgiveness.
Remove malice from your own heart, And behold!
The whole world is your friend.*

SIKHISM

*When the sinner findeth himself wholly detached
and freed from all save God, he should beg
forgiveness and pardon from Him. Confession of sins
and transgressions before human beings is not
permissible, as it hath never been nor will ever be
conducive to divine forgiveness. Moreover, such
confession before people results in one's humiliation
and abasement, and God — exalted be His
glory — wisheth not the humiliation of His
servants.*

BAHA'I

FRIENDS

One should pick one's associates from among the wise and the good. Evil associates will corrupt a man. A man who reproves intelligently should be sought out since his words are the advice one needs.

BUDDHISM

Evil companions corrupt good morals. Shun those who are not good. The wise man will seek out those who will help him to become better and attain greater sanctity. Shun the idle and the unproductive and seek out the industrious and the creative.

CHRISTIANITY

Seek out the company of those who can give good advice and whose example is good. One may be friendly to all men, but one should be discriminating in one's choice of associates. Good associates will do you good, therefore cling to the best.

CONFUCIANISM

Look upon all the living beings as your bosom friends, for in all of them there resides one soul. All are but a part of that Universal Soul. A person who believes that all are his soulmates and loves them all alike never feels lonely.

HINDUISM

*Avoid those who do wrong. To associate with the
wicked is to cast suspicion upon oneself. Therefore,
avoid such suspicion by seeking out only the
good men as associates.*

ISLAM

*Do not allow yourself to be deluded by evil associates. Make
friends with those who are considerate
both towards other people and towards animals.*

JAINISM

*Do not follow the path of the wicked or associate
with those who are evil. Good friends are best.*

JUDAISM

*Friend, if you possess some good, let us be friends,
Let us be partners for doing good, And let us
ignore each other's flaws.*

SIKHISM

*The good should associate with those whom they
can help. A virtuous man will radiate his virtue
far and wide. One is fortunate to be the associate
of such a good man.*

ZOROASTRIANISM

It is incumbent upon everyone to show the utmost love ... and sincere kindliness unto all the peoples and kindreds of the world, be they friends or strangers.

BAHA'I

GIVING

Liberality is a virtue. The wise and good man will share what he has with others. In this way he will save himself. Giving is saving.

BUDDHISM

One should give to all who ask, for in giving to the needy one gives to God. The Christian should bear the burdens of others and should share his goods with those in need. The Lord loves a cheerful giver.

CHRISTIANITY

Benevolence is a characteristic of the wise. The superior man gives generously to the needy. He knows that this is the chief element in humanity.

CONFUCIANISM

Giving with cheerfulness is the way to security and happiness. Giving is superior to receiving since the giver acquires a friend and protects himself from enemies. The wise man will always share with others.

HINDUISM

The pious man will give alms. His gifts will return to him. God loves the giver. As God has been generous to man, so should he be generous to his fellow beings.

ISLAM

Charity without fellow-feeling is like sowing a fallow land.

JAINISM

Those who have should give to those who have not. The poor should always be helped. One who gives to the poor gives to the Lord. If one does not give when the poor ask, one will not be aided when one is in need.

JUDAISM

Be generous to all creatures, both human and animal. Long life is the reward for generous giving.

SHINTO

Only what one gives to others will be preserved for him in the future world. The generous will find contentment.

SIKHISM

One should help all those who are in need, and should not think of his reward. The good will be frugal in order to be liberal to those in need.

TAOISM

The Wise One was generous. So should all His followers be generous. For one who helps the poor does in so far help to make the Lord King.

ZOROASTRIANISM

To give and to be generous are attributes of Mine; Well is with him that adorneth himself with My virtues.

BAHA'I

GOLDEN RULE

*Remember that you are like other men. As you
fear and suffer, so do they. Therefore, do not do
those things which will cause them trouble. As
you would not harm yourself, do not harm others.
Whatever you would want men to do to you, do
even so unto them. One should love his neighbour
as himself.*

CHRISTIANITY

*What one does not like to have done to himself, he
should not do to others. The rule of philanthropy
is to draw one's self a parallel for the treatment of
others.*

CONFUCIANISM

Behave with others as you would with yourself.

HINDUISM

*Anas told that when God's messenger said: "Help
your brother whether he is acting wrongfully or
is wronged," a man asked, "Messenger of God, I
help him when he is wronged, but how can I help
him when he is acting wrongfully?" He replied:
"You can prevent him from acting wrongfully.
That is your help to him."*

ISLAM

One should treat all beings as he himself would be treated. Since all beings hate pain, he should kill nothing.

JAINISM

What you hate, do to no man. One should love his neighbour as himself.

JUDAISM

As you sow, so shall you reap; This body is the result of your actions.

SIKHISM

Do not do unto others all that which is not well for yourself.

ZOROASTRIANISM

The principle of fairness, often called the Golden Rule, is common to all religions. Baha'u'llah has re-emphasised this spiritual law in this way: "Lay not on any soul a load which ye would not wish to be laid upon you, and desire not for any one the things ye would not desire for yourselves. This is My best counsel unto you, did ye but observe it."

BAHA'I

GUIDANCE

*Trust in the Lord and He will guide you aright.
One who has this trust need fear nothing. He can
be at perfect peace and happiness, for he will be
guided aright.*

BUDDHISM

*If we trust in God, He will carry us through all
hardship and troubles. One should have complete
confidence in God. Even in persecution we should
not falter, for God will guide us to our reward.*

CHRISTIANITY

*God is with the good man. Therefore, he should
never fear. God will guide the good aright. Follow
the will of God without questioning, for it is true
and the end will be success.*

CONFUCIANISM

*No enemies can overcome the believer. He trusts
in God, knowing that God will guide him through
all troubles.*

HINDUISM

The Lord has created and will guide man through life. Those who trust in His guidance at all times will find that the Lord will not fail them.

ISLAM

From the roots, grows up the trunk of the tree, from the trunk, shoot up the branches; out of them grow the twigs and the leaves, and then there are produced flowers, fruits and juice. Similarly, obedience to the guidance of Jina is the root of the tree of religion and the liberation is the highest resultant (juice). It is through His guidance that one achieves immortal renown and abiding peace.

JAINISM

Trust in God at all times. He will lead you even through the shadows of death and will protect you in the presence of your enemies.

JUDAISM

Be not led astray by the illusion of the world, (And know then that) without the Guru, no one is ferried across (the sea of existence). The Guru shows the Path to the strayers. Sing then the Lord's praise, for This alone is thy eternal duty.

SIKHISM

God is our protector and guide. In Him must we trust and never waver. He is all powerful and will never fail those who yield to His guiding.

ZOROASTRIANISM

Religion confers upon man eternal life and guides his footsteps in the world of morality. It opens the doors of unending happiness....

BAHA'I

HAPPINESS

The wise and good man will be happy in this world and in the next. He has the secret of perfect contentment and joy. One should not seek after happiness, but should find it as a natural result of good deeds.

BUDDHISM

The Christian life is a happy one. Despite persecution and tribulations, the Christian is happy because he has right on his side and his reward will be great in heaven.

CHRISTIANITY

Even in the most meager of circumstances, the man who lives rightly will be happy. Ill-gotten gains will never bring happiness. Heaven grants happiness to the good.

CONFUCIANISM

True happiness comes not from external things, but through attachment to things spiritual. It is an inner joy which nothing outside can destroy. It comes from God and is a reward for goodness. Only the wise have real happiness.

HINDUISM

Happiness will come when one turns to God and seeks union with Him. The good will be rewarded greatly for their works and will be happy.

ISLAM

Happiness comes through self-control. The man who is able to subdue himself will find happiness in this and in the next world.

JAINISM

Judaism is joyous. One who has the Lord on his side should be happy, rejoicing all the time. Happiness results from good works. If people keep the law, they shall be happy.

JUDAISM

Virtue goes hand in hand with happiness.

SHINTO

We shall find happiness in the worship of the Lord. He made everything and is the source of all true happiness.

SIKHISM

Human happiness comes from perfect harmony with one's fellow beings. The source of divine happiness is complete accord with God. The good shall be truly happy.

TAOISM

Holiness is the source of the truest happiness. Only those who live justly shall know happiness. The unrighteousness of man shall bring misery.

ZOROASTRIANISM

Happy are they who understand; happy is the man that hath clung unto the truth, detached from all that is in the heavens and all that is on earth!

BAHA'I

HATE

Hatred is damaging to mankind. One who gives way to hatred is no longer master of himself.

BUDDHISM

Love and not hatred should rule. If one has any hatred in his heart, he should cast it out before turning to his religious observances. To hate is to be a murderer.

CHRISTIANITY

Those who speak harshly will stir up hatred. One should demand much of himself and little of others. By so doing one will avoid hatred.

CONFUCIANISM

Hatred breeds confusion. Clear thinking and careful action can come only when the heart is free from hatred.

HINDUISM

Abu Ayyub al-Ansari reported God's messenger as saying: "It is not allowable for a man to keep apart from his brother more than three days, the one turning away and the other turning away when they meet. The better of the two is the one who is the first to give a greeting."

ISLAM

Hatred will drag down the soul and defile it. To attain purity of soul, one should avoid hatred at all costs.

JAINISM

It is wrong to hate a brother. Hatred begets strife, and strife destroys a people. Only the fool will give way to hatred.

JUDAISM

Return goodness for hatred. The wise man hates not, but seeks always to do good. He will not enter a dispute and thus can have no one disputing and hating him.

TAOISM

*He whose mind is imbued with the One alone
feels not jealous of another.*

SIKHISM

*Blessed are such as hold fast to the cord of
kindliness and tender mercy, and are free from
animosity and hatred.*

BAHA'I

HOME

*The home should be a place of mutual understanding
and love, of chastity and faithfulness, of
reverence for the aged and respect for the young.
There should be no selfishness among members of
the family.*

BUDDHISM

*In the home the child should honour his father
and mother and the parents should respect the
children. The parents' duty is to teach the
children and rear them in the truly religious life.*

CHRISTIANITY

*The home, with its atmosphere of love and
respect, should be the model for the entire world. At
all times, affection, harmony, and honour should
reign in the home. Filial piety, begun in the home,
extends to the state and becomes devotion to
the ruler.*

CONFUCIANISM

*The highest law of the home is fidelity among its
members. The wife should be faithful, the children
obedient, and the father understanding and
industrious. Thus will develop the perfect home.*

HINDUISM

*Prayer should dominate the home. In it the parents
and children should serve the Lord at all times.
The home is a unit and should approach the
Lord as one. Here kindness to parents should
dominate the children and the parents should see to
it that the children are nurtured rightly in all
religious matters.*

ISLAM

*The child should support his father and mother
when he is able to do so and they are in need. But,
in religious matters, the man must stand alone.*

JAINISM

*The home should be a place of worship. Here all
members should serve the Lord and honour and
respect should reign. The home in which
righteousness rules will stand against the world and
the children going out from it shall prosper and
receive bounteous rewards.*

JUDAISM

*Yes, such a householder is Pure, like Ganga's
water.*

SIKHISM

The home should be a place where obedience, peace, love, generosity, humility, truth, and righteousness reign. Here children should respect their parents. To such a home will come contentment, knowledge, prosperity, and glory.

ZOROASTRIANISM

My home is the home of peace. My home is the home of joy and delight. My home is the home of laughter and exultation. Whosoever enters through the portals of this home must go out with gladsome heart. This is the home of light; whosoever enters here must become illumined.

BAHA'I

IMMORTALITY

*The good and wise will find happiness in the life
to come. The evil and thoughtless will die eternally.
Heaven is a place of bliss for the good. Here one
who has lived earnestly and wisely shall find his
reward.*

BUDDHISM

*God has prepared a home after death for the good.
All here on earth changes and passes away, but he
who obeys the will of God lives forever. Heaven is
a place of rewards and hell a place of punishment.
Each man shall receive justice after death.*

CHRISTIANITY

*The soul destroys the earthly body in order to
make for itself a new and more beautiful body. The
wise man will become immortal. Death is the
taking off of the robe of life to put on the robe of
immortality. The good and just shall live forever.*

HINDUISM

*The good and those who have died in the service
of the Lord shall be rewarded with eternal life.
God will gather all his faithful followers to
himself after death. Theirs is the reward of Paradise.*

ISLAM

*There will be a life hereafter. The evil shall go to
hell and the good to heaven. In heaven the soul
develops to perfection.*

JAINISM

*The dust will return to dust, and the spirit of man
will go to its everlasting home. The Lord will
reward the good with eternal life and the spirit of
man will dwell forever with God who made it.*

JUDAISM

*The good man dies only to go home. He does not
die, but lives forever. Heaven is the company of
the saints.*

SIKHISM

*Death is a going home. The good and wise shall
suffer no harm even though the body dies.*

TAOISM

*The righteous shall live happily in the future life
while the evil shall suffer great torments. The
Lord dwells in the life beyond to receive His
followers.*

ZOROASTRIANISM

It is evident that the loftiest mansions in the Realm of Immortality have been ordained as the habitation of them that have truly believed in God and in His signs. Death can never invade that holy seat. Thus have we entrusted thee with the signs of thy Lord, that thou mayest persevere in thy love for Him, and be of them that comprehend this truth.

BAHA'I

JUSTICE

The wise man will weigh matters carefully so that he may judge justly. Hasty judgement shows a man to be a fool.

BUDDHISM

All judgements should be made justly. Beware lest you fall into evil judgements. God is just and will judge all men justly, according to their deeds.

CHRISTIANITY

The man of honour desires justice and will seek after it in all his actions. Only the fool is unjust.

CONFUCIANISM

The one who hurts pious men falls victim to his own designs. This is divine justice.

HINDUISM

Live a just and honest life. God does not do injustice, and he expects his followers to be just. Act justly at all times and under all conditions.

ISLAM

*God, let me not stray away from the path of
justice. I may remain ever steadfast against the
denunciation by others; should ever be unmindful
of the prospects of immediate death or life
through millenniums, keeping my equanimity in
poverty and plenty.*

JAINISM

*The Lord loves justice and has erected his throne
upon it. The man who deals justly with his fellow
beings at all times shall truly live.*

JUDAISM

*Injustice shall be overcome by justice. If one has
made a promise, he must fulfil it justly even
though it be made with the unrighteous. Man
should think and act justly at all times.*

SHINTO

Our acts, right and wrong,
At Thy Court shall come to judgement;
Some be seated near Thy seat,
Some ever kept distant;
The toils have ended of those,
That have worshipped Thee;
O Nanak, their faces are lit with joyful radiance,
And many others they set free.
We are saved not,
If thoust judge according to our actions,
Forgive us, O Thou Forgiver of all,
And lead Nanak across this ocean of life.

SIKHISM

To see justice and fail to do it is an act of
cowardice.

ZOROASTRIANISM

O Son of Spirit! The best beloved of all things in
My sight is Justice; turn not away thereform if
thou desirest Me, and neglect it not that I may
confide in thee. By its aid thou shalt see with
thine own eyes and not through the eyes of others,
and shalt know of thine own knowledge and not
through the knowledge of thy neighbour. Ponder
this in thy heart; how it behoveth thee to be.
Verily justice is My gift to thee and the sign of
My loving kindness. Set it then before thine eyes.

BAHA'I

LOVE

One act of pure love in saving life is greater than spending the whole of one's time in religious offerings to the gods, sacrificing elephants and horses.

BUDDHISM

Love is supreme in Christianity. It is the heart of religion. God's love for man and man's love for God, the love of man for man, and the love of the Christian for all others are central themes of Christian teaching.

CHRISTIANITY

Love makes a spot beautiful; who chooses not to dwell in love, has he got wisdom? Love is the high nobility of Heaven, the peaceful home of man. To lack love, when nothing hinders us, is to lack wisdom. Lack of love and wisdom lead to lack of courtesy and right and without these man is a slave.

CONFUCIANISM

The Lord is the lover of all beings, but he especially loves those who keep his laws and are devoted to him. One can best worship the Lord through love.

HINDUISM

Abu Dharr said: God's messenger came out to us and said: "Do you know which action dearest to God is most high?" When one man suggested prayer and Zakat and another Jihad, the Prophet said: "The action dearest to God most high is love for God's sake."

ISLAM

One should show compassion to all creatures and obey the Law at all times.

JAINISM

One should love God with all one's heart. And one should love his neighbour. The stranger has a claim on one's love. God loves the good man, the righteous. He also loves the sinner and seeks to draw him from his sin and to himself.

JUDAISM

The Lord will visit the home where love reigns. Love is the representative of the Lord.

SHINTO

One who loves God truly will be cleansed of all his impurities. We obtain salvation by loving our fellow beings and God.

SIKHISM

God's love is for the good man at all times. The Wise One taught universal love towards one's fellow beings and His followers should follow His teaching.

TAOISM

Everyone should love virtue. Man is the beloved of the Lord and should love Him in return.

ZOROASTRIANISM

In the world of existence there is no greater power than the power of love.

BAHA'I

MAN

*Man is the product of his thinking. All that he is,
all his ideals, likes and dislikes, his very self, is
the result of thought.*

BUDDHISM

*Man is a little lower than the angels. He is the
measure of all values. It is for him that the world
was created and for him Jesus came to earth and
died. Man is God's workman on earth. If man
fails, all fails.*

CHRISTIANITY

*Heaven has made man good. His original nature
is good, but many depart from it. The earthy in
man pulls him down and away from Heaven.
Those who follow the heavenly part of themselves
are great, while those who follow the earthy
part are evil.*

CONFUCIANISM

*Man is the highest of animals. He is an animal
with an immortal soul which cannot be hurt by
the world. There is nothing nobler than humanity.*

HINDUISM

God created man to sit on His throne on earth.
Man is God's viceroy on earth.

ISLAM

Man is a creation of God, made in the likeness of
God. He has been made a little less than the
divine. As sons of the living God, men are clay in
the hands of God, the potter, to do with as he
wills.

JAINISM

Most people are enamoured of pleasure and do
not reach the moral heights possible for man. The
self is the foe to greatness and is as dangerous as
pride, anger, and greed. The self is to be subdued.

JUDAISM

Man's body is the dwelling place of God. God is
the soul of man, his eternal nature.

SIKHISM

Man is both human and divine. The divine in him
is eternal and of infinite worth. The human may
pass away, but the divine is everlasting. His
goodness comes from God.

TAOISM

The Wise One created man to be like Him. The mind of man enclosed in a body comes from the divine. Thus, man should serve only the good and flee from all that is wicked.

ZOROASTRIANISM

Man is the supreme Talisman. Lack of a proper education hath, however, deprived him of that which he doth inherently possess.

BAHA'I

MEDITATION

Great are the rewards of contemplation. One who trains himself in the art of meditation will penetrate the heart of truth and discover great spiritual riches.

BUDDHISM

Thinking on the great things of life results in greatness. If one would be good, one must contemplate the good. All virtues will be strengthened by meditation upon them. This, too, is the way to clearer understanding.

CHRISTIANITY

One should avoid bad, evil thoughts. One should at all times think that which is good. Careful consideration of the end as well as the beginning and the middle will save one much trouble.

CONFUCIANISM

Those who do not meditate can have neither steadiness nor peace. The great and the wise meditate constantly on the divine. This is the source of strength and the way to knowledge of the Supreme One.

HINDUISM

Meditate upon God and you will find peace.
Meditation must be in humility and constant if
one would reap its true rewards.

ISLAM

Contemplation is the means of obtaining stability
of mind. Even though one is severely persecuted,
one must obey the law of silent meditation.

JAINISM

Meditation brings understanding. One should
contemplate God in all His greatness at all times.
This is enjoyable and brings the greatest peace
and happiness. To meditate upon the Law of the
Lord is the duty of all believers.

JUDAISM

Just as there is fragrance in the flower,
And reflection in the mirror,
Similarly, God lives within;
Search Him in thy heart, O brother.

SIKHISM

To a mind that is "still" the whole universe
surrenders.

TAOISM

Keep the plan and purposes of the Lord always in mind. Meditate upon them day and night. Then you will come to a clear understanding.

ZOROASTRIANISM

Meditation is the key for opening the doors of mysteries. In that state man abstracts himself; in that state man withdraws himself from all outside objects; in that subjective mood he is immersed in the ocean of spiritual life and can unfold the secrets of things in themselves.

BAHA'I

OBEDIENCE

Those who obey the law and follow studiously the commandments shall have serenity of mind, joy, and prosperity. Obedience is the way to the good things of this life and of the life to come.

BUDDHISM

The true Christian is known by the fact that he obeys the commandments of God. If one desires true life here and hereafter, he should keep the commandments. The Christian will obey God at all times rather than man. If one keeps God's commandments, God will dwell in him and act through him.

CHRISTIANITY

To obtain the favour of Heaven, one should observe all the statutes of Heaven. Those who reverently observe these statutes and are obedient to the will of Heaven shall have happiness and shall become men superior.

CONFUCIANISM

The laws of God are eternal, lofty, and deep. The man who is obedient to them will be happy and after death will experience joy unsurpassable.

HINDUISM

All shall be well with the believer who hears the word of the Lord and obeys. The law of the Lord has been set down for man to read and obey. The punishment for disobedience is severe.

ISLAM

The fool refuses to obey the Law and is sorry when he reaches the hour of death. Man is created to fulfil the law of God. The wise and pious are always obedient to the law of God.

JAINISM

The commandments of the Lord are just and should be obeyed. To disobey God will result in punishment, to obey will result in happiness and blessedness. God will show no mercy to those people or nations who refuse to obey.

JUDAISM

Man is to God what a servant is to his master. Thus, he should obey at all times. If he obeys he will have honour and happiness and will eventually meet his master.

SIKHISM

The complete and perfect man is the one who obeys the will of the Lord at all times.

TAOISM

The Lord is wise. Thus, what he orders is good for his followers and his commandments should be obeyed. Immortality is the reward he offers to the obedient.

ZOROASTRIANISM

O Son of Man! Wert thou to speed through the immensity of space and traverse the expanse of heaven, yet thou wouldst find no rest save in submission to Our command and humbleness before Our Face.

BAHA'I

PEACE

*True happiness comes to those who live at peace
with their fellow beings. The aim of all should be
to learn peace and live peacefully with all men.*

BUDDHISM

*Jesus is the Prince of Peace. He came to this earth
to bring peace to all men. The peacemaker is
blessed and shall be a child of God. We should
seek the way of peace and finally come to peace
with God.*

CHRISTIANITY

*Seek to live in harmony with all your neighbours
and at peace with thy brethren. Peace and love
should reign throughout the world. The Most
High God seeks peace among his people.*

CONFUCIANISM

*If one would find happiness and security, one
must seek for peace. The peaceful mind will
become established in wisdom. God is a god of
peace and desires peace for all people.*

HINDUISM

God will guide men to peace. If they will heed him,
He will lead them from the darkness of war to the light of peace.

ISLAM

The enlightened will make peace the foundation of their lives. All men should live in peace with their fellow beings. This is the Lord's desire.

JAINISM

Judaism looks forward to an ideal time when peace shall reign throughout the world. God commends peace and urges all His followers to work for peace. The peaceful life offers the greatest opportunity for happiness and prosperity.

JUDAISM

The earth shall be free from trouble and men shall live at peace under the protection of the divine.

SHINTO

The True Nam is my support;
It is my food and drink;
By it my hunger of every kind is satisfied.
By saturating my mind, it has satisfied all my
longings,
And given me peace and happiness.

SIKHISM

The wise esteem peace and quiet above all else.
The good ruler seeks peace and not war, and he
rules by persuasion rather than by force.

TAOISM

All men and women should mutually love one
another and live in peace as brothers and sisters,
bound by the indestructible hand of Humanity.

ZOROASTRIANISM

Today there is no greater glory for man than that
of service in the cause of the 'Most Great Peace'.
Peace is light whereas war is darkness. Peace is
life; war is death. Peace is guidance; war is error.
Peace is the foundation of God; war is a satanic
institution. Peace is the illumination of the world
of humanity; war is the destroyer of human
foundations.

BAHA'I

REPENTANCE

Whatever faults one may have, one should confess them and seek forgiveness. Confession is a necessary part of repentance.

BUDDHISM

All men are sinners. Therefore, they should repent, confess their sins, and seek forgiveness of God who is ready always to forgive those who are truly repentant.

CHRISTIANITY

Whenever a person is in the wrong, he should hasten to confess his error and make amends.

CONFUCIANISM

To the extent that one has sinned, one should confess and earnestly beg God's forgiveness and mercy. If one does this, God will hasten to forgive and wipe away one's sins.

HINDUISM

The Lord is quick to forgive those who confess their sins and turn to Him for forgiveness. One who has sinned should seek the Lord with a repentant heart. He will surely find mercy.

ISLAM

*Repent of pleasures and instruct others to do so.
If one lives only for the present, and does not
prepare for the future, one will repent later on.*

JAINISM

*If one hides his sin and does not confess it, he
shall not prosper. God is willing and anxious to
forgive the man who confesses his guilt and truly
repents.*

JUDAISM

*Relinquish your sins and have recourse to good
actions,
Repent if you have committed any sin.*

SIKHISM

*If one has made a confession of his sins and does
earnestly resolve never to sin again, he shall be
forgiven. The religion of the Wise One takes away
the sins of those who confess.*

ZOROASTRIANISM

Beseech thou the One true God that He may enable everyone to repent and return unto Him. So long as one's nature yieldeth unto evil passions, crime and transgression will prevail.

BAHA'I

SINCERITY

Be not slothful or flippant, but be earnest at all times. Goodness comes from earnestness. God loves the earnest, sincere man.

BUDDHISM

One's religious actions should not be for showing but should be done in earnestness. At all times the true Christian is sincere and earnest. He is never the hypocrite who acts merely for show.

CHRISTIANITY

Whatever you do, you should do with all your heart. Heaven will help the man who is sincere, and one's fellowmen will trust him if he is sincere and earnest.

CONFUCIANISM

The Lord does not favour those who are not sincere and honest.

HINDUISM

God is not to be fooled. He knows whether or not a man is earnest in his professions and will deal with all men according to this knowledge. One who repents in earnestness will be forgiven.

ISLAM

Clear thinking comes through sincere and earnest effort. One can be proficient in religious practices only to the degree that one is earnest and sincere. Through sincere actions one becomes pure.

JAINISM

The Lord will help those who are earnest. He is near to the sincere and knows man's inner being. He is not fooled by outward appearances.

JUDAISM

Sincerity is the single virtue that binds divinity and man in one.

SHINTO

To pretend religion is of no avail. Earnestness is the only basis for true religious acts.

SIKHISM

The manner of heaven is earnestness. If one is sincere and earnest in one's acts, one will attain to the truest sainthood.

TAOISM

As long as a man is earnest, his reward will be great.

ZOROASTRIANISM

Honesty, virtue, wisdom and a saintly character redound to the exaltation of man, while dishonesty, imposture, ignorance and hypocrisy lead to his abasement.

BAHA'I

WAR

Intentional killing of any living being is condemned. Peace, and not war, is the ideal and should be sought by all who are truly religious.

BUDDHISM

The peacemakers, and not the warmakers, are blessed. Those who take the sword shall perish by the sword. War is the road to destruction, while peace is the road to happiness and prosperity.

CHRISTIANITY

God desires peace, not war. Everyone should strive to dwell in peace with his fellows. The man subdued by force is in his heart still rebellious, but one who is won by love will be loyal forever.

CONFUCIANISM

Causing injury to any creature is wrong. The wise man will seek always to avoid strife and will dwell in peace. The ideal for life here on earth is peace, not war. No one should seek to extend his power through war.

HINDUISM

Peace is to be sought by all. If there is war the religious man will seek to establish peace. The Lord has ordained peace, and no one can engage in war without endangering the stability of the world.

ISLAM

Never kill anything for any reason whatsoever. The wise live at peace with all men, whatever the cost. War is totally condemned.

JAINISM

Only fools give way to war. The wise seek peace. The peace-loving, the meek, shall inherit the earth. The Lord will judge between nations, and wars are of no avail.

JUDAISM

Let the land under heaven enjoy peace and be free from war. The Sun-Goddess will protect the country so that it may live at peace.

SHINTO

When all efforts to restore peace prove useless
and no words avail, lawful is the flash of steel
then
And right it is the sword to hail.

SIKHISM

War is always followed by disastrous years. He
who truly serves as a ruler of men will not lead
his nation into war. Arms are unblessed and are
full of sorrow.

TAOISM

War is the greatest crime man perpetrates
against man.

ZOROASTRIANISM

When a thought of war comes, oppose it by a
stronger thought of peace. A thought of hatred
must be destroyed by a more powerful thought of
love. Thoughts of war bring destruction to all
harmony, well-being, restfulness and content.

BAHA'I

WEALTH

Wisdom and self-mastery are true wealth.
Material possessions are not real wealth, for
they can be taken away from a man. Real wealth
is everlasting.

BUDDHISM

Moth and rust will corrupt earthly treasures.
Therefore, real treasures are heavenly, where
nothing can destroy them. One's heart will be
with one's treasures. Therefore, turn from
mammon to God. Do not count the wealth of
this world as valuable. The only true value lies
in spiritual wealth.

CHRISTIANITY

Prosperity comes from Heaven. Wealth gained by
unrighteousness will not last. The only true
wealth is that which comes through right acting.
Too often riches are accompanied by pride and
other evils.

CONFUCIANISM

One should work constantly and seek after
wealth. But, if one gains wealth, one should share
it with those in need. Beware lest wealth shut the
door on the good life. Riches are but means to
doing good and should not become the goal of life.

HINDUISM

Wealth should be employed at all times for the things of the Lord. He who wastes his wealth in evil actions is condemned. Wealth must not be allowed to turn one from service to God.

ISLAM

Wealth is fleeting and will never completely satisfy anyone. To put faith in wealth is to be a fool, for it will cause pain both in this world and in the next.

JAINISM

Trust not in wealth. It is fleeting and may be the cause of much evil and suffering. The poverty of a good man is more to be prized than the wealth of the evil man. If one has wealth, one should use it for good and not for evil.

JUDAISM

In prosperity many come and surround a man When fortune frowns at him, all abandon him and nobody comes near. Of what use is wealth, amassed by wrongful means?

SIKHISM

One's person is of more value than all of one's wealth. Therefore, one with wealth must beware lest one sacrifice oneself for his wealth. Riches acquired unjustly will become poison to the soul.

TAOISM

Prosperity and wealth are the rewards of right living and come from the Wise Lord. Thus, wealth must be employed in the service of the Lord.

ZOROASTRIANISM

The essence of wealth is love for Me; whoso loveth Me is the possessor of all things, and he that loveth Me not is indeed of the poor and needy. This is that which the Finger of Glory and Splendour hath revealed.

BAHA'I

WORK

Works, and not birth, determine one's place in the world. At all times one should work diligently and with earnestness. Hard work is praised.

BUDDHISM

God works and so man should work. The Christian will be diligent in good works all the time, for a man is to be judged by his works. As man works for the good, it is God who works in and through him.

CHRISTIANITY

Not ease, but work is the mark of a good man. The superior individual does not indulge in luxurious ease, but works constantly for the good. He is superior in that he does things which the base cannot understand or appreciate.

CONFUCIANISM

One becomes what he does. The man who does good becomes good, and the man who does evil becomes evil. The motive of one's works should not be the consequences. One should do good despite the results. No one who does good will come to an evil end.

HINDUISM

Everyone should strive to excel in good works.
Work constantly. God will observe your works
and judge you according to whether they are good
or evil.

ISLAM

A day once gone will never return. Therefore, one
should be diligent each moment to do good. We
reach the goal of the good life by pious works.

JAINISM

God will judge each man according to his works.
All men shall be known by their works. Whatever
one undertakes to do, one should to it with all his
might. God commands men to work and promises
that He will be with them in all good works.

JUDAISM

God has determined from the beginning the works
man must do. No man can escape this determination.
Men become saints or sinners by their works only,
not by their professions. Good works bring men to
a clear knowledge of the divine.

SIKHISM

We come to the divine through our good works.
Thus, at all times man should strive to work well
so that he may gain recognition in the eyes of the
Wise Lord.

ZOROASTRIANISM

It is enjoined upon everyone of you to engage in
some form of occupation, such as crafts, trades,
and the like. We have graciously exalted your
engagement in such work to the rank of worship
unto God, the True One.

BAHA'I

WRATH

A true disciple is free from all passion, including wrath. To give way to wrath is to bind oneself to a master who will destroy. Happiness lies in freedom from wrath.

BUDDHISM

Everyone should beware of wrath. Do not become angry without cause. Love, and not anger, is the mark of a true Christian. Put away all wrath and malice and seek to dwell in friendliness with all men.

CHRISTIANITY

Do not deal with your fellow beings as though you were superior to them. Those who do will find themselves hated. To avoid the wrath of others, demand little of them and much of yourself.

CONFUCIANISM

Wrath breeds confusion. One who would be master of himself and of all situations must avoid wrath. The ideal is to live free from hate and anger.

HINDUISM

*Abu Huraira told that a man asked the Prophet to
give him some instruction and he said: "Do not be
angry." The man repeated that several times and
he replied: "Do not be angry."*

ISLAM

*Wrath is a passion which defiles the soul. The
wise man will avoid wrath lest he be caught in the
toils of the passion as a fly is caught in glue. Even
though he is beaten, the religionist will not give
way to wrath.*

JAINISM

*The wise man is slow to wrath. He gives soft
answers and thereby turns away wrath on the
part of others. Love, and not wrath, should be the
goal of all true believers, for wrath leads to strife.*

JUDAISM

*Wrath is the cup, filled with worldly love, and pride
is the server. Through excessive drinking in the
company of falsehood and avarice, the
mortal is ruined.*

SIKHISM

Return goodness for hatred. Do not become angry and do not quarrel with your fellow beings. The wise man is free from wrath at all times.

TAOISM

If a man exercises his anger and wrath against the blood-thirsty tyrants who are like ferocious beasts, it is very praiseworthy; but if he does not use these qualities in a right way, they are blameworthy.

BAHA'I

The Press & the Public hail the Book of the Year

The quotations compiled are indeed illuminating and useful in promoting tolerance and understanding.

—Rajiv Gandhi

Unity in Diversity will be a great catalytic agent in promoting unity, national integration and fellow feeling among the millions of our countrymen.

—Arjun Singh, M.P.

I have read the compilation with great interest and I feel sure that it will be a significant contribution to the strengthening of our society and the promotion of world unity.

—Dr. S. Gopal,
Jawaharlal Nehru Memorial Fund

Unity in Diversity is a bouquet of flowers gathered from gardens of different religions, good for the soul.

—Anoop Singh,
Advocate, Supreme Court of India

Permit me to congratulate you for this work, which shall live forever.

—Prof. Fida M. Hassnain

The book is worth its weight in gold and a prized possession.

—R.K. Dubey

This admirable book should receive wide circulation.

—Dr. Karan Singh

Unity in Diversity is an excellent anthology. Its designing and production are superb.

—Prof. S.C. Dube

It is the only book in recent years which I have read with interest from the first page to the last in one sitting. Your work is a laudable endeavour at this critical juncture of the country's history and an eye-opener to fanatics.

—Raghunadha Rao,
Professor of History, S.V. University, Tirupati

The book is indeed very attractively produced and should be of value to teachers and students involved in the study of programmes of national and cultural integration.

—Dr. Prem Kirpal

Your initiative in this regard is welcome and timely. It is high time that we defused the highly surcharged atmosphere by pointing to the essentially peace-loving message from all the world's religions.

—Dr. Mohinder Singh

After looking into your book my confidence in Indian secularism was enhanced and I thought that we can survive any crisis so long as persons of your cadre are active.

—**Muhammad Iqbal,**
Printest, New Delhi

This volume will be of immense guidance and help to teachers, parents and enlightened citizens throughout the world.

—**S.P.Ruhela,**
Jamia Millia Islamia

I expect that this book will serve as a Handy Bible for every young man who would like to have a ready reference of religious knowledge in a scientific way.

— **Prof. V. Narayankaran Reddy**

I congratulate you on bringing out such an imaginative and timely compilation. The authorities concerned should enable the students of today to read it so that they have some ideals to seek as citizens of tomorrow.

—**T.N. Chaturvedi,**
Comptroller & Auditor General India.

As regards your publication Unity in Diversity, I can only say how impressed I am with it. It is a fine collection of some of the noblest thoughts expressed by our thinkers and saints, presented with elegance and beauty at a time when they are most needed.

—**L.K. Jha**

The book is beautifully produced, excellently designed and admirably displayed. It is a book which should be on all reference shelves, at home and in libraries.

—**Raj Gill,**
The Hindustan Times

Amidst such a bristling atmosphere, O.P. Ghai's Unity in Diversity comes as a soothing balm on frayed nerves.

—**Kalpita C. Sarkar,**
The Patriot

In these days when discussion is centered round a new education policy books like this will go a long way in inculcating the spirit of love and brotherhood among the younger generation.
—**The Mountain Path**

To a world which has been and continues to be a witness to religious strife and bloodshed, to people who are living on the brink of a nuclear war bred by distrust and intolerance of one another, the contribution of a book like Unity in Diversity is undoubtedly immense.
—**Indian and Foreign Review**

When the stress and strain of life make one angry, dejected or rebellious one will undoubtedly derive comfort from Mr Ghai's compilation.

—**The Statesman**

Artistically and lavishly produced, this book, dedicated to the cause of inter-religious unity, contains a choice selection from the notings of the author emphasising the oneness of the underlying wisdom.

—**The Advent**